HEART AND MIND
—— OF A ——
CHAMPION

Are You Ready for the Battle?

PERNELL STONEY

PAGE PUBLISHING, INC.
New York, NY

First originally published by Page Publishing, Inc.
2018

ISBN 978-1-64138-904-4 (Paperback)
ISBN 978-1-64138-905-1 (Digital)

Printed in the United States of America

INTRODUCTION

TODAY BELIEVERS LACK the knowledge of the power they have been given and the effect it has on their and others' lives. Tragically, this lack of knowledge is taught daily on television shows, in movies, in the streets, at home, in the media, and yes, in some churches. We are teaching our sons and daughters in ways that are contrary to what the Bible tells us, even the use of negative language. This way of life comes from a lack of understanding the power we have in God. The bottom line, Satan has deafened our ears and blinded our eyes to what God's Word has told us to do.

However if we, as God's people, would accept Him, and study His Word, we would come to know that the things we say and do determine who we will become. Currently, the lifestyle we live is a defeated one; we are letting the devil defeat us in the battle. This is far from honoring God. As men and women of God, we need to renew our thought patterns through the Word of God. Then His Word will teach us the ingredients we need to honor Him and act and speak positively with boldness.

Until then, our children will continue to be lost because they don't see the Spirit of God and the heart of a champion in their parents or their friends. All of us, while here in the flesh, need to get filled with the Spirit of God.

This book will present you with Scriptures from the Old and New Testaments that will prove to you that God wants you to be positive and have a heart and mind of a champion. It also shows the importance of your actions based on speaking and developing a relationship with Him and loving one another. As you read my eye-opening, life-changing experience, I hope it will change you the way it has changed me. I pray to God that you will hear what He is saying to you and can experience the great joy of being open and obedient to our Lord and Savior, Jesus Christ. After all, God did not make a mistake, and you are just who you were when you were born.

ACKNOWLEDGMENTS

FIRST, I GIVE thanks and honor to my Lord and Savior, Jesus Christ, for it is through His blood that I am saved; to my wife, Hwason, a true friend and woman of God, for still loving me after forty years of bad and good times; to my daughter, Cherry, one of the sweetest people you could ever meet, who is always thinking of others first; and to my son, Steven, a man with strong family values, who is always in my heart with a love that is unmatched.

In addition, I would like to thank my spiritual families: Minister Johnny Williams, Robin Williams, and Moses Williams, who have mentored and supported me for the past twelve years. Pastor James, Gigi, and DD Williams, thanks for your friendship; we love you with the love of God. God has given all of you a heart of love and care; thank you for being there for us.

Thanks to Dr. Michael and Brineta Mitchell, my mentor and longtime friends of Restoration Ministries International (RMI) Christian Fellowship in Augusta, Georgia, for teaching us the Word of God.

To Dr. Ron and Sue Rockwell, our pastors and spiritual leaders at Harvest Church in Phoenix, Arizona, thanks for being an example of not only teaching, but living a spiritual life the seven years I attended Harvest Church in Arizona. Thanks for teaching us how to love one another the way God wants us to. Special thanks go to apostle John Evans for letting me know it was not my fault, but it was my time.

Also, special thanks go to my new pastors, Mirek and Linda Hufton of World Harvest Church in Roswell, Georgia, who boldly teach the Word of God, letting us know how to be strong and bold in the Word of God. Following the great commission to take the gospel to the four corners of the world.

Again, thanks to all our friends. Remember, God loves you, and so do we.

Chapter 1

MY TESTIMONY

MY MOTHER GAVE birth to me in a small town in South Carolina, the last of four brothers and one sister. I was told my mother died when I was six months old; they did not say from what, just that she died. I was not raised with my siblings; I lived with an aunt. Two brothers went to live with another aunt, and my oldest brother and sister went to live with our grandmother. I was told this happened because our father took off and left. No one could take all of us in, so we were split up among relatives that helped and took us in. When I was about eight years old, I went to live with my grandmother; by this time, I had picked up some bad habits: stealing from people, coming in late, hanging out with the wrong kids. These kids were much older than I was.

1. Things did not change when I went to live with Granny. My grandmother was in

her seventies and not welll educated, she worked in the cotton fields for the majority of her life. But there were six things she taught you:

2.   To Love and respect others no matter what your situation or circumstances may be. She showed loved to all of us.

3.   She taught us how to be a giver and a provider. She provided a warm place to stay.

4.   She taught us how to work hard (she provided three hot meals every day).

5.   She taught us how to pray, give thanks, and trust God. After teaching us to pray, she would listen to us pray every night at bedtime.

6.   She took us to church every Sunday.

7.   She taught us that hard work built strength. I remember at the age nine, every morning about 6:00 a.m., I was getting on a truck heading to the cotton fields, watermelon fields, or the peach orchards to pick cotton, load watermelons on trucks, or pick/grade peaches. Let me tell you, none of them were easy. If you wanted to make more money, you had to really work hard. I would make twenty-five to thirty dollars a week if I really hustled and work hard.

When Sunday came, and it was time to go to church, my grandmother did not play; she would not accept excuses on why you could not go to church. If you missed church trying to fool her you were sick, she would keep you in the house. You could not go outside for a few days until she felt you were well again.

I still hung out with the wrong boys. I started smoking cigarettes—yes, cigarettes—at the age of nine. As I got older, I started drinking wine every once in a while. I would drink some white lightening. I did not have much clothing. I had one suit—and that was my church suit—and one pair of church shoes. My regular school shoes had two holes in the bottom. I had to walk around any water on the ground to not get my socks wet. The jeans you see people wearing today with all the holes in them? That was how I went to school every day. Back then, that was not the style and was not cool. To add to the embarrassing feeling, Granny would patch some of the holes with different color of material. Some days, I went to school looking like a clown. She did not have money to buy me good clothing; once in a while, she would take me to the secondhand store (today I believe it is call the thrift store) to get some clothes.

At the age of twelve, I got caught by the store owner stealing a can of Vienna sausage; instead of calling the police or my grandmother, which would have been worse than calling the police, he offered me a job. He said, "Son, stealing is not good. If you want something, work for it." Looking back at things, God was looking after me.

When I was a freshman, there was a guy that would bully me every day, teasing me on how I look, what I was wearing, punching me. Someone told my brothers what was happening to me. We did not live in the same house. The only time I did get to see them was at school or on weekends. My brothers told me I had better start standing up for myself and fight back. Now I had never been in a fight before. The word got out that this boy was going to beat me up after school. My brother told me I had better fight, and if I lost, he was going to beat me too. He said, "We will be there to see the fight." When he said he would beat me too if I lost, it did not faze me because being the youngest, I was always getting beat up by my brothers any way. But that was different than being beaten by a stranger. What really fired me up and gave me the boldness to stand up to this bully was they said they would be there; to me that meant they had my back if thing got out of hand.

Well, after school, we met, and all the kids surrounded us; we were in the middle. We squared off. The guy came charging at me. I closed my eyes and, through an overhand, left and hit him in the eye. He stopped. When I opened my eyes, he was holding his eye, bent over. Everyone was saying "Get him, get him." And it was on. I jumped on him and went left, right, left, right—he was on the ground. My brother had to pull me off him. From that day on, I never had a problem with anyone else in school trying to bully me.

I share this testimony because it sets the stage for what this book is about. The next six chapters will reveal the bully we face every day and know he has already been defeated. Knowing we have the power and authority that was given to us by the father. Getting the spirit, mind, and body operating as one we become champions, ready to stand our ground, ready for the battle that the enemy brings to us daily.

Chapter 2

VISION

IT TOOK ME a long time to realize I was going down the wrong road. I was being led by the blind, not knowing anything about what the word of God said. Yes, I went to church, but the church I went to was not a teaching church; it was a preaching church, and back in those days, preachers would do a lot of screaming and humming. As a young kid, I really did not get anything out of what was being said. I don't remember going to a Bible study. But I will tell you this, it was a shouting and screaming church. I am not sure if the church had vision or not, but I do know there was a lot of shouting going on. I did hear a few sermons on the prodigal son, Daniel in the lion's den, and the three Hebrew boys. These were the only teachings I understood at the time growing up. I can tell you this, the things I did not have or the things I received from my grandmother gave me the foundation I needed to build my relationship with the Father. What little I got out of church service also made a difference because seeds were planted. And now it gives me a burning desire inside that if I ever get on my feet to take care of myself, I would never have shoes with holes in the bottom or wear pants with holes or patches over the holes. I truly thank God for what I went through growing up. After studying the word, I now know I had a vision back when it was in that fistfight, it was to win and not lose.

Saints, brothers and sisters of God, we must read his word to know he is on our side, he will protect us. We must see it and embrace it in our hearts. His word tells us where there is no vision, the people perish; but he that keepeth the law, happy is he. No, we are not under the law but under grace; we still need to be obedient to the law. Visualize standing your ground in this battle, which is what our Lord and Savior wants us to do. You may say, "Why are we standing our ground and what ground are we standing?" I am glad you ask.

The first thing you must know is that the war has already been won; the devil was defeated by our Lord and Savior when he died on the cross, went to hell for our sins, defeated the devil, and rose on the third day. So that being said, why are you still fighting someone that has been defeated? What we need to do now is stand and protect what was given back to us. We were given a second chance, and with that second chance, we were given the Holy Spirit to lead and guide us in all that we do or need to do. In the book of Habakkuk 2:2, it tells us to write the vision and make plain upon the tablets. Proverbs 29:18 tells us where there is no vision, the people perish, but he that keepeth the law, happy is he. The war has been won, but we are confronted every day with a battle of some kind that the devil is trying to put on us. No one is exempt from the day-to-day battles; we all have them. We must see ourselves victorious in our daily battles.

The weapon we need to use in our daily battles is the word of the God. You will always lose the fight if you don't use the correct weapons, and you will not know what weapon to use until you go to the word. You need to visualize your victory in the battle, write it down, and know the weapons we need to use are prayer, faith, trust, belief, and love. Constantly showing in the fruits of the spirit, building up your most holy faith in the Lord. It is so important to have a vision, just as when I was in school when I was challenged by a bully. When my brother confronted me and gave me an ultimatum, which was to lose and get beat again. My vision was win, and I would be free from being bullied. The vision I had was being a winner, well the same principle applies in the word of God. We must stay in training every day to prepare ourselves for wiles of the devil. Remember, we are not perfect, but we serve a perfect God.

To continue my testimony, after graduating high school, I went to live with my older brother in Corona, New York. My cousin got me a job at a box factory where he worked. I started hanging out with my brother's friends, who were much older than me. Drinking, smoking gambling. Every Friday and Saturday night, we were at a different person's house, drinking and gambling. Never went to church. This went on for several years. Doing that several years' time frame, I got married, and we had a son. I still kept doing the things I did before I got married. After two years, my marriage fell apart, and my wife left me. I lost my family, I lost my job; now I was alone with all kinds of bad thoughts going through my head. One day, I was playing music and drinking, and the devil was attacking me from all sides with things to do. I was living in the projects on the sixth floor in Flushing, New York. The devil really had me on the ropes. I stood up from my sofa and went to the window. I could hear the devil. "You have nothing to live for, you lost your family and your job, you can't pay your rent, you are going to get put out. You have nothing to lose, just jump and end it now." I opened the window, and when I did, I heard someone say "Stop feeling sorry for yourself and live, read your Bible." Now there were no one in the apartment except me, but this voice was very soft. So I stopped, closed the window and sat down on the sofa, picked up the Bible, and began to read.

The more I read the word, the clearer my vision became; at that time, the vision was to live and not die. Things in my life would change, not knowing how but trusting in the word of God. In 1974, I entered the army, and things would not be the same again. My life began to change spiritually, but I was fighting a fleshly battle trying to control my flesh. I was still doing some of the bad habits I picked up. But while in basic training, we were given the opportunity to go to church. I took full advantage of that, and I have never looked back. Did I do everything right after that? No. But I was being groomed and trained to have the heart of a champion. It has taken many years of people praying for me, reading His word, being in the company of men of God, being obedient, and listening to God. Know that the battle is still not over, but I am more equipped than years past. I was given a mission to tell my testimony and minister to men. My vision/mission is to point men (young and old) to my Lord and Savior (Jesus Christ) for the opportunity to be saved by grace. As long as God gives me strength, I will be bold in speaking his word to whoever will listen. That is why it is so important to write the vision down and look at it every day. It will take work on your part to bring the vision to reality. When God gives you something, you must visualize it, seeing yourself accomplishing what God has put in your spirit.

I believe a vision is like a sports game; all champions do what it takes to prepare for each phase of the game. The Holy Spirit is your coach for your vision; if you follow the instructions of the coach, you will make the vision a reality. I believe every living soul has a mission (vision) to accomplish here on earth. Look deep into your heart; God has put a passion in there for you. Write it down and go pray about it. You must also know who you are, because this makes a very big difference in living out your vision. The Holy Spirit will confirm what you have been given.

Chapter 3

OBEDIENCE

Put on the Armour of God

WHEN WE SPEAK about putting on the armor of God, most of us don't know what it means. Well, I will try to break it down for you so you will have a better understanding. You need that understanding when you are going into a battle. You can read about the armor of God in Ephesians 6:10–17.

> Finally, my brother, be strong in the Lord and the power of His might. Put on the whole armour of God, that ye may be able to stand against the wiles of the Devil. For we wrestle not against flesh and blood, but against principalities, against the spiritual wickedness in high

places. Wherefore take unto you the whole armour of God, that ye may be able to withstand in the evil days, and having done all, to stand [this is where having a heart of a champion will pay off, standing the ground that was given to you]. Stand therefore, having your loins grit about with TRUTH. What truth are they talking about well, I am glad you asked. (Ephesians 6:10–14; emphasis mine)

Jesus said unto him, I am the way, the **TRUTH**, and life no man cometh unto the Father but by me. (John 14:6; emphasis mine)

Also John 15:1 tells us Jesus is the TRUE vine. Now you know when you grit your loins with truth, you are stripping on Jesus.

And your feet, shod with the Preparation of the Gospel of Peace. (Ephesians 6:15)

The question is who is our peace? I have the answer, John 14:27 "**Peace I leave with you, my peace I give unto you**." Not as the world giveth, give

I unto you. Let not your heart be troubled neither let it be afraid.

> Above all, taking the **SHIELD OF FAITH** [what faith]? Wherewith ye shall be able to quench all the fiery darts of the wicked. (Ephesians 6:16)

Whose faith are we talking about in this verse? I am glad you ask. We are talking about your faith in Jesus Christ. Your victory is based on your faith in our Lord and Savior. This is what it tells us in **Galatians 2:16**: "Knowing that a man is not justified by the works of the law, but by the faith of Jesus Christ. Even we have believed in Jesus Christ, that we might be justified by the faith of Christ, and not by works of the law: for by the works of the law shall no flesh be justified."

When our faith is unshakable, we are able to stand up to the evil that is brought to our doorsteps every day. Having the heart of a champion is having faith is Jesus Christ, knowing that the victory is ours.

> And take the **HELMET of salvation, and the SWORD of the SPIRIT**. (Ephesians 6:17)

The helmet of salvation is to protect and give deliverance from danger or suffering. The sword of the spirit is the word of God; when we read/study it and apply to our life, we receive what it says we can have. Through our relationship with Christ, we have the victory. Remember, study to show thyself approved unto God, a workman that needeth not to be ashamed, rightly dividing the word of truth. II Timothy 2:15 Also, remember II Timothy 1:7, "For God hath not given us the spirit of fear, but POWER and of LOVE, and of a SOUND MIND."

We can only receive this through our faith in Jesus Christ. Having a heart of a champion gives you the ability to overcome your daily battles. Remember this, when you walk out your door, you should have on Jesus, for He is your strength in time of weakness, He is your healer in time of sickness, He is your comfort in time of loneliness, He is your help in your time of need, He is your victory in time of war, and He is your joy in time of sorrow.

We must stay on our knees praying and giving thanks always for all He has done and still doing in our lives. We must connect our spirit with his spirit and let him lead us. A champion knows he can't win the battles alone. We must follow the plan of God and His plan for all his children, the one's that accept Him as their Lord and Savior.

When you get ahead of your guide or the one that is leading you, you will get lost, and that is when all the bad decision are made, because we are trying to make them our self and not letting the Holy Spirit lead us. His word say: "Howbeit when he, the Spirit of truth, is come, he will guide you into all truth: for he shall not speak of himself; but whatsoever he shall hear, that shall he speak: and he will shew you things to come," John 16:13.

Remember you were created to be a champion and ready for any battle. So stand up and be counted. Your father has given you the power to defeat the tricks of the devil. We must wear all the weapons in God's armory.

Chapter 4

PRAISING, PRAYING GOD'S WAY THINGS TO KNOW

QUESTION 1: WHAT *is God telling us about prayer? I will ask you this same question at the end of this chapter.*

What is prayer: *A spiritual communion with God or an object of worship, as in supplication, thanksgiving, adoration, or confession? Also: A devout petition to God.*

1. Read Luke 11:1, "Lord, teach us to pray," Luke 11:6–8, *Three things God tells us to do: (1) ASK; (2) SEEK, and (3) KNOCK._*
2. James 5:16 tells to confess your faults one to another, and pray one for another, that ye may be healed. The effectual fervent prayer of a righteous man availeth much.

a) "Watch ye therefore, and pray always, that ye may be accounted worthy to escape all these things that shall come to pass, and to stand before the Son of man" (Luke 21–36). *What are all these things? Living in careless ease, cursing, drinking, lying, stealing, a disobedient spirit that keep us occupied with the problems of this life.*

b) **NOTE:** *We must have action with our request. The word tells us that Faith without action is dead.*

c) "And He spoke a parable unto them to this end that men ought always to pray and not to faint" (Luke 18:1).

d) **1 Thessalonian 5:17** *(pray without ceasing)* for this is God's will for you who belong to Christ Jesus.

QUESTION 2: Are we praying the way he wants us to pray? I would say no, we are not praying the way he wants us too. Now you are saying "yes, I am." Well, let me tell you a few things, and then you decide if you are praying the way God wants you to pray.

1. Have you humbled yourself before God?
2. Are your prayers being answered?

3. Are you praying for others or are you complaining about what they are doing or not doing?

4. Are you praying for the lost/unsaved?

5. Are we blessing those who curse us and spitefully use us (Luke 6:28)?

6. Have you forgiven your brother, your friend, your neighbor, your coworker, your boss, your wife, your children? Are you still holding a grudge? I believe if you think hard enough, you will find something. (Matthew 18:21, 22, "give us instructions on forgiveness"). A warrior has the heart of a champion; they are always in the war room, in their prayer room. They know the battle is won in the spirit.

"If my people, which are called by my name, shall humble themselves, and pray, and seek my face, and turn from their wicked ways; then will I hear from heaven, and will forgive their sin, and will heal their land" (2 Chronicles 7:14).

He is only asking us to do four things:

1. *Be humble.*
2. *Pray.*
3. *Seek his face.*
4. *turn from our wicked ways.*

Politicians wants you to believe they can change things to make it better. Well, if you believe them, you have not read the Bible. To be more specific, they have not read 2 Chronicles 7:14, which gives us the instructions to change what is happening in the world today.

If we want to see results, we must pray God's way. As one writer said, those who stay on their knees can stand up to anything. This is what champions do so they can stand up to those small battles that, if not dealt with, will turn into wars.

The word of God is telling us, "Where there is two or three gathered together in my name there I am in the midst of them. *How often are we in two or three?"*(Matthew 18:18–20).

Now why do we need to have two or three to pray? Well, you don't need others to pray, but I am going to give you the best reason I know why you should.

a) Because God is telling you if there are two or three, he is in the midst. Also, if there are two or three, you are praying in agreement. When this happens, there is no stopping what God will do for you. I learned a few days ago that relationships are the conduit of life. We need to build a relationship with our Lord and savior Jesus Christ.

b) Two are better than one, because they have a good reward for their labor (Ecclesiastes4:9). In *The Living Bible,* it states, *"two can accomplish twice as much as one. For the results can be much better."*

c) Ecclesiastes 4:12 says "and one standing alone can be attacked and defeated, but two can stand back-to-back and conquer; three is even better, for a triple-braided cord is not easily broken."

d) Brothers, we need to humble ourselves. Seek the father together and ask to cleanse our hearts and take praying seriously. Team up. I would ask you to triple up with each other and pray at least once a week for fifteen to twenty minutes together. Not to pray for ourselves, but to pray for others.

e) Our life will turn around when we begin to pray for others, just like Job. His life did not turn around until he prayed for his friends. We've got to do it God's way if we want answers to our prayers.

f) Remember, we were saved by grace. He loves us; we just need to be obedient to his word (Ephesians 2:8). We need to remember who we are and what we are here for. *Ephesians 2:10 tells us who we are.*

g) You don't always have to say something to receive something from God. Let me explain. When you study his word, meditating on it day and night, when you do all that is written, you are asking to be blessed. When you lead someone to Christ, you are asking for a blessing. When you help the poor, you are asking to be blessed. When you give thanks to him, he knows your heart; you are asking to be blessed. When you say kind things to others and about others, you are asking to be blessed.

h) *Finally,* my brothers, we must be obedient to the word of God and pray to him the way he has laid out for us. He said "there hath no temptation taken you but such as is common to man" 1 Corinthians 10:13"

i) *The flip side of this is if you don't pray God's way, you will fall into temptation.*

j) *Remember the five Ds: DISGUISES, DISTORT, DIVERT, DENY, DISCREDIT.*

Now, I would ask you to look inside yourself and ask, "Have I let these things slip into my though pattern, creating negative vibes for others. Have I dropped my guard down, creating a weak spot for the devil to get in?" The heart of a champion is all ready to defend, because he knows whom he belongs to.

NOTE: *We must be aware of whom and what we are dealing with in high places. Another reason why we should follow what God has laid out about praying.*

How many of you have a GPS in your phone or your car?

How many of you want a free GPS?

What kind of coordinates are you putting in it?

What does a GPS do? This is a navigational system that man has developed to get you from one point to another, using the shortest route possible to get you there.

What does GPS stand for? I believe it stand for "global positioning system." They are not reliable. Sometimes it will lead you down a dead-end road; sometimes it will just stop working.

I want to tell you about another navigational system that was purchased for you a long time ago. Champions are using it all the time. It is never wrong. It is the most accurate system ever created. It is call GOD'S POSITIONING SYSTEM (Proverbs 16:9). Better known as the *Holy Spirit.* He was given to us to use, all we have to do is accept Jesus Christ as our Lord and savior and follow God's instructions on praying. Be faithful in our prayer life, activating our GPS spiritually that will help you navigate through the mess in the road of life. I said I would ask you this question at the end of this chapter: *Are you praying God's way?*

Praises and Worship

This book is about what we do and what we don't do that gives us the heart and mind of a champion.

We all must take time to give God praise and worship Him. I don't think we worship or praise him enough.

What is praise? It is to make a noise: the joy God's people have in Him, which is expressed in praise.

Why should we praise Him: Because he is our _____ and _____ (savior), we owe all to Him.

Below are some scriptures that support why we should praise our savior. Men, we are leaders and teachers, we must set the example for the next generation to follow. Stand up and make a difference; remember we are a family.

> We will not hide them from their children, showing to the generation to come the praises of the LORD, and his strength, and his wonderful works that he hath done. (Psalm 78:4)

> And now shall mine head be lifted up above mine enemies round about me: therefore

> will I offer in his tabernacle sac-
> rifices of joy; I will sing, yea, I
> will sing praises unto the LORD.
> (Psalm 27:6)

If you want to stage a jail break from the Prison you are in (the problems, situation and circumstances) all you have to do is trust and believe in God's word and put it in action. Check out what happen to Paul and Silas in Act 16:25–26.

> And at midnight Paul and
> Silas prayed, and sang praises
> unto God: and the prisoners
> heard them. 26, And suddenly
> there was a great earth quake, so
> that the foundation of the prison
> were shaken and immediately
> all the doors were open, and
> every one's bands were loosed.
> (Acts 16:25)

Note: you can read the rest of the chapter, I just wanted you to see what happens when you praise the Lord from the standpoint of your situations. He inhabits the praises of his people.

> But ye are a chosen gen-
> eration, a royal priesthood, an
> holy nation, a peculiar people;
> that ye should show forth the

_____of him who hath called you out of darkness into his marvelous light. (1 Peter 2:9)

By him therefore let us offer the sacrifice of _____to God _____, that is, the fruit of our lips giving thanks to his name. (Hebrews 13:15)

Whoso offereth _____ glorifieth me: and to him that ordereth his conver-sation aright will I show the sal-vation of God. (Psalms 50:23)

We as men of God owe it to our families to always give God praise. He inhabits the praises of His people.

Worship

What is worship? It is giving honor to where honor is due.

Who and why are we worshiping? We are wor-shiping our Lord and Savior Jesus.

Because of what He has done for us, and also because he is our savior, our creator, and our redeemer. We should praise and worship Him always.

But the hour cometh, and now is, when the true worship-

pers shall _____the
Father in spirit and in truth: for
the Father seeketh such to worship him. (John 4:23)

If you want to receive from the Father, you need
to give Him P_____ and W_____. We
as married men and single men, we need to do what
God intended for us to do. We are to L_____
and T_____. This is what you must do to make
a deference. When we walk into a room, the climate
should change. This will let you know it is all because
you are being obedient to God's word.

> God is a Spirit: and they that
> worship him must worship him
> in spirit and in truth. (John 4:24)

When we realize how important worshiping our
Lord and Savior, we will do it more often, building a
closer relationship to our Savior. We are commanded
to put no other God before God.

> Then saith Jesus unto him,
> get thee hence, Satan: for it is writ-
> ten, thou shalt W_____
> the Lord thy God, and him only
> shalt thou serve. (Matthew 4:10)

Finally, my brothers, let us dig deep and activate
the Holy Spirit that is within us. Now that you know

what his word tells us. If your heart is not right, read Psalm 51:10 "Create in me a clean _____, O God; and _____ a _____ _____ with in _____."

Remember, when the praise goes up, the blessings come down. A sample of this is in the book of Acts 16:25–34. Here are two men with a *heart of a champion*, knowing what to do and how to go about doing it. This is what I call the God kind of faith, which is heart faith and not head faith. At midnight, Paul and Silas prayed and sang praises unto God, and the prisoners heard them. *Note: the prisoners heard them (hearts of champions), having no concern about who heard them. Their mind was fixed on God.* And suddenly there was a great earthquake, so that the foundations of the prison were shaken, and immediately, all the doors were opened, and everyone's bands were loose.

We must always keep our mind fixed on God; he is the author and finisher of our faith. The mind and *heart of a champion* knows how and when to worship our Lord and savior. When Jesus died on the cross, he gave everyone the opportunity to become champions. He even left instructions for us to follow to build up spiritual strength and walk with our head up prepared for any battle. All we must do is have faith in his instruction, carrying them out as he has outlined in his word. The mind and heart of a champion knows the importance of following instruction. This is what makes them champions. Give Him praise and worship daily and see how your life will change.

Praise and Pray Always

"By him therefore let us offer the sacrifice of praise to God continually, that is the fruit of our lips giving thanks to his name" (Hebrews13:15). "Giving thanks always for all things unto God and the Father in the name of our Lord Jesus Christ" (Ephesians 5:20). Psalm 150, praising the Lord. I believe we have forgotten that we are to praise God; he smiles when we praise him. Praise him. It opens the door to his blessings. Prayer/praying: we must do this all the time, which is what the word tells us to do. We must realize it is two parts to receiving the blessings of the Lord. Luke 18:1, "And he spake a parable unto them to this end, that men ought always to pray and not faint."

The word *faith* means "to not fall away, not to give up." When we look around, we see many have given up and grown weak in standing their ground for the word. (*More scriptures: Ephesians 6:18, 1 Thessalonians 5:17, and James 5:16.*) As you can see, we need to have balance in our spiritual life. Just praying, we are like a bird with one wing; but when we add praise in, we can soar on the wings of God's blessings. We also let him know by saying *Glory to God*; *bless the Lord*; *thank you, Jesus*; *Praise the Lord*; and *Hallelujah*.

There Is an Art of Praying

In my study on prayer, I learn there are many different prayers, and we should study the word to learn what it is saying and how to use it. We are to use it the way God intended for it to be used. This was very important for me; now I can pray the way God wants us to pray. Now I can share this with you to help you as the spirit has led me. The number one thing was when we pray we must ask the **Father** in the name of **Jesus**. John 16:23–24, "And in that day ye shall ask me nothing. Verily, verily, I say unto you whatsoever ye shall ask the **father** in *My Name*, he will give it you (emphasis mine)." This is telling me that if I want anything from the **father**, I must ask for it in **Jesus's** name. This is very important. I was praying all wrong. This insight has given me a better understanding on how to pray and get my prayers answered.

I was also reminded that men are to always pray (Luke 18:1). That means I need to be praying all the time, not when things happen and I need something. It also tells me in Ephesians 6:18, "Praying always with all prayer and supplication in the Spirit, and watching thereunto with all perseverance and supplication for all saints." I should not just pray for my family, but for all to come to Jesus as their Lord and Savior.

I also learned seven steps to getting your prayers answered. There could be more, but these were brought to my attention. For me, it is just what I needed to know. Knowing this put me in line with praying God's way.

1. Decide what you want from God. God is a precise God.
    a. Mark 5:28
    b. Mark 10:51
2. Find scriptures that promise the answer to what you are asking for. When you do this, you are standing on the promise of God. I believe this is what gets your prayers answered.
    a. John 5:14–15
3. Get them planted in your heart, because this where the true man lives. Remember, out of the abounded of the heart, the mouth speaks.
4. Ask God for your desires.
    a. John 15:7
    b. John 16:23
    c. Matthew 7:7–8
5. Believe you receive (Mark 11:23). I learned not to let martial pictures cause me to fail.
6. Refuse to doubt. Only make positive statements of faith (Philippians 4:8).
7. Meditate on God's promises (Proverbs 4).
8. Give thanks and praise always (Philippians 4:6).

As I stated before, this has been a very enlightening study. It has really opened my eyes to how important prayer is. The different types of prayers make a big difference on getting your prayers answered. Also, having faith in the promises of God and believing you will get what you ask for in the name of Jesus to the Father.

I would recommend this class to anyone, or should I say, everyone. Because the word tells us we don't know not how to pray. I truly thank God for all that he has taught me during this course, and I will pass it on.

Chapter 5

FAITH

WE ARE LOSING the battle because we don't have the God kind of faith. You may be asking yourself what kind of faith is that? Well, I am glad you are asking this question. This tells me two things, one you don't have it, and you need to know it in order to overcome defeat. Faith is a part of our life. We can't live without it. Everything we do, we do it by faith. What puzzles me is when it comes to having faith in God, we are lacking, we doubt, we show signs of unbelief. But we can get in a car and have all kinds of faith that the car will take us where we want to go. Which lets me know we have faith in material things rather than having faith in the spiritual things of God. This also lets me know we are not ready for our daily battles. If you are not ready for the daily battles, you will not be ready for the war. When the fight is a spiritual one, and there is no faith, it will be very difficult to have a heart of a champion. Faith is a key element to having the heart of a champion. The God kind of faith is a spiritual faith that comes from the heart. The kind of faith most of us have is a natural kind of faith that comes from the head. We must physically see it before we believe it. This type of faith will not get you the promise or the benefits of God.

What is faith? Now faith is the substance of things hoped for, the evidence of things not seen (Hebrews 11:1).

Let us break it down a little more, by giving you four examples of the God kind of faith. I will give you the chapter, you must find the verses; this will help you in your study and memory of what you are reading about.

Example 1: *The lady with the blood issue for twelve years. She believed if she could but just touch the hem of Jesus's, garment she would be healed.* You can read it in Mathew 9:_____?

Example 2: *Daniel* was a man of strong faith. Knowing whom he served, he had no fear of what man would do to him. Because he did not obey the decree not to petition any other God, Daniel prayed three times a day to his God, not thinking about what man could do to him. Knowing what his God could and would do for him if he would be faithful and trust him, he has victory. The heart of a true champion, you can read about this in the book of Daniel 6:_____?

Example 3: There were three young Hebrew boys, Shadrach, Meshach, and Abed-nego. They were told they had to worship a golden image that the king had set up. They refused to do that, and they were bound and thrown into the fiery furnace. This is the God kind of faith we all need. They were not afraid of fire because they knew whom they served, whom they belonged to. You can read the whole story in the book of Daniel 3:_____?

Example 4: The centurion's servant is healed. A centurion came to Jesus saying "Lord, my servant lieth home sick of the palsy" (paralytic/relaxing of the nerves of one's side/disabled, weak of limb). Grievously tormented, Jesus said, "I will come and heal him." The centurion told him just speak the word and he will be healed. Jesus said, "I have not found so great faith." You can read the story in the following books and chapters: Matthew 8:_____, Luke 7:_____.

I gave you just a few example of real faith, the God kind of faith that we all should have. Having the heart of a champion will give you the hope that you need to attach your faith on. Increasing faith in the spiritual and decreasing the natural faith (head faith)—the thing you only see, which is not faith.

Now let us find out why it is so important to have faith as a Man of God.

The Importance of Faith

1. Without faith, it is impossible to please him.
    a. Hebrews 11:6
2. Faith is the lifestyle of the believer.
    a. Romans 1:17
    b. 2 Corinthians 5:7
    c. 1 Timothy 6:12
3. We receive salvation by faith.
    a. Ephesians 2:8

How to Obtain Faith

1. Faith comes by hearing the message.
    a. Romans 10:17
2. Hearing faith for physical healing.
    a. Acts 14:1–10
    b. Mark 5:25–34

Faith or Mental Assent

1. Mental assent is based on your sense
    a. John 20:19–29

2. Faith is based on Father God's Word
    a. Romans 4:17–21

"For he that cometh to God must believe that he is, and that he is a rewarder of them that diligently seek him" (Hebrews 11:6).

Now that we know the importance of faith, we must activate it in our life. We must have *faith*, *hope*, *trust*, and *belief* in God's word.

"If ye shall ask any thing in my name, I will do it" (John 14:14).

All of this really depend up on this scripture: John 15:7. "If ye abide in me, and my words abide in you, ye shall ask what ye will, and it shall be done unto you."

Now that we know this, let us abide in His word just like it tells us in Joshua 1:8.

Finally, my brothers, God has given everyone a measure of faith. Let us activate what He has given us.

"For I say, through the grace given unto me, to every man that is among you, not to think of himself more highly than he ought to think; but to think soberly, according as God hath dealt to every man the measure of faith" (Romans 12:3).

So stop asking God to increase your faith, and start acting on what he has already given you. Then you will see your faith grow.

In the book of Luke 17: _____, the apostles said unto the Lord, "increase our faith." This is what he told them, "If ye had faith as a grain of mustard seed. You might say unto this sycamine tree, be thou pluck up by root, and be thou planted in the sea; and it should obey you."

What I am telling you is trust his word and begin acting on it. Remember, faith is an action word. You must move on what he has given you and let him do the rest. When we don't do our part, he can't do his part. Let me give you an example. You are going to have a test in a few days. The teacher gives you a chapter to read, and the questions for the test will come from the chapter. You don't read the chapter, but you ask God to help you pass the test. Well, he can't help you pass the test because you have not done your part. You did not study, you did not prepare for what you wanted.

I believe faith works in the same way. God has given you the faith for everything you need that is in line with his word. Trust his word, believe his word, and act upon his word. The heart and mind of a champion know this and act upon it; therefore, they have victory in their battles.

Chapter 6

BECOMING THE MAN AFTER GOD'S OWN HEART

1 Samuel 13:5–14
Acts 13:22
1 Samuel 15:2–26

THEN THEY ASKED for a king; and God gave them Saul the son of Kish, a man of the tribe of Benjamin, for forty years. And when he had removed him, he raised up David to be their king; of whom he testified and said, 'I have found in David the son of Jesse **a man after my heart,** *who will do all my will'* (Acts 13:21–22; emphasis mine).

Do we aspire to become the men and women after God's own heart? It is easy to romanticize the lives of the saints; however, when you consider the dealings of the Lord in David's life and the lives of all the saints, we see something very different.

Consider David and all the qualities we admire in him. Was David born with these traits? Did such things come natural to him? No. Rather, all these things came about because of God's grace. Like all the saints, David was subject to—and willingly accepted—the Lord's discipline in his life.

Consider the language in the above verses. Note the language used. First we read of King Saul. Recall how Saul gave the impression of being humble, but he was proud. Yet, as he began his reign, the Lord gave Saul a "new heart" (spirit). The people noticed the difference in Saul, but then the tests came—two of which proved critical. In the thirteenth chapter of the first book of Samuel, we read of the first test.

> And the Philistines mustered to fight with Israel, thirty thousand chariots, and six thousand horsemen, and troops like the sand on the seashore in multitude; they came up and encamped in Michmash, to the east of Beth-a'ven. When the men of Israel saw that they were in straits (for the people were hard pressed), the people hid themselves in caves and in holes and behind rocks and in tombs and in cisterns, or crossed the fords of the Jordan to the land of Gad and Gilead. Saul was still at Gilgal and

all the people followed him trembling. He waited seven days, the time appointed by Samuel; but Samuel did not come Gilgal, and the people were scattering from him. So, Saul said, "Bring the burnt offering here to me, and the peace offerings." And he offered the burnt offering. As soon as he had finished offering the burnt offering, behold, Samuel came; and Saul went out to meet him and salute him. Samuel said, "What have you done?" and Saul said, "When I saw that the people were scattering from me, and that you did not come within the days appointed, and that the Philistines had mustered at Michmash, I said, "Now the Philistines will come down upon me at Gilgal, and I have not entreated the favor of the LORD; so, I forced myself, and offered the burnt offering." And Samuel said to Saul, "You have done foolishly; you have not kept the commandment of the LORD your God, which he commanded you; for now, the LORD would have established your kingdom over Israel forever.

But now your kingdom shall not continue; the **LORD has sought out a man after his own heart;** and the LORD has appointed him to be prince over his people, because you have not kept what the LORD commanded you. (1 Samuel 13:5–14; emphasis mine)

Saul had an army of men whom he had personally hand-picked. And yet we see the real courage of these men when it came to a test. For the most part, they scattered and hid. As more men deserted him, Saul became more and more anxious, until finally, he took matters into his own hands and, going against God's command, did not wait the full seven days. Consequently, Saul was not established in his kingdom.

I believe this how we act; we don't give God time to act before we start taking things in our hands. Thinking we can take care of it, we end up messing things up worse. We must learn to have patience, which is one of nine gifts of the spirit.

Sometime later, the second crucial test came. The Lord commanded Saul to take his army and destroy the Amalekites. Again, we read this in the first book of Samuel.

Thus says the LORD of hosts, 'I will punish what Am'alek

did to Israel in opposing them on the way, when they came up out of Egypt. Now go and smite Am'alek, and destroy all that they have; do not spare them, but kill both man and woman, infant and suckling, ox and sheep, camel and ass.' So, Saul summoned the people, and numbered them in Tela'im, two hundred thousand men on foot, and ten thousand men of Judah. And Saul came to the city of Am'alek, and lay in wait in the valley. And Saul said to the Ken'ites, 'Go, depart, go down from among the Amalekites. And Saul defeated the Amalekites, from Hav'ilah as far as Shur, which is east of Egypt. And he took Agag the king of the Amalekites lives, and destroyed all the people with the edge of the sword. But Saul and the people spared Agag, and the best of the sheep and of the oxen and of the fatlings, and the lambs, and all that was good, and would not destroy them; all that was despised and worthless they destroyed. (1 Samuel 15:2–9)

Here we see how Saul obeyed the Lord—but only as far as it suited him. While he did destroy much of the Amalekites, he did not destroy everything. Rather, he saved the best and destroyed what the scripture calls "despised and worthless." When the prophet Samuel appeared on the scene, Saul tried to convince him that he had indeed done God's will. However, it was clear to the prophet that he had not. Samuel could hear the sheep that Saul had spared. Saul tried to excuse himself by shifting the blame on others; however, it did not work.

> The word of the LORD came to Samuel: 'I repent that I have made Saul king; for he has turned back from following me, and has not performed my commandments.' And Samuel was angry; and he cried to the LORD all night. And Samuel came to Saul, and Saul said to him. 'Blessed be you to the LORD; I have performed the commandment of the LORD.' And Samuel said, 'What then is this bleating of the sheep in my ears, and the lowing of the oxen which I hear? Saul said, "They have brought them from the Amalekites; for the people spared the best of the sheep and of the oxen, to sacri-

fice to the LORD your God; and the rest we have destroyed.' Then Samuel said to Saul, 'Stop! I will tell you what the LORD said to me this night.' And he said to him, 'Say on.' And Samuel said, 'Though you are little in your own eyes, are you not the head of the tribes of Israel? The LORD anointed you king over Israel. And the LORD sent you on a mission, and said, 'Go, destroy the sinner, the Amalekites, and fight against them until they are consumed.' Why then did you not obey the voice of the LORD? Why did you swoop on the spoil, and do what was evil in the sight of the LORD?' and Saul said to Samuel, 'I have obeyed the voice of the LORD, I have gone on the mission on which the LORD sent me, I have brought Agag the king of Am'alek, and I have destroyed the Amalekites. But the people took of the spoil, sheep and oxen, the best of the things devoted to destruction, to sacrifice to the LORD your God in Gilgal'... And Samuel said to Saul, 'I will not return with you; for you have

> rejected the word of the LORD,
> and the LORD has rejected you
> from being king over Israel.
> (1 Samuel 15:10–21, 26)

Because of Saul's incomplete obedience, the kingdom was taken from him, and the Lord replaced Saul with David.

Consider again the verses in the book of Acts concerning David, and let us see if we can learn why the Lord chose David to succeed Saul.

> Then they asked for a king;
> and God gave them Saul the
> son of Kish, a man of the tribe
> of Benjamin, for forty years.
> And when he had removed him,
> he raised up David to be their
> king; of whom he testified and
> said, "I have found in David
> the son of Jesse *a man after my
> heart, who will do all my will*"
> (Acts 13:21–22)

Saul was the people's choice. He was tall, handsome, and humanly speaking, certainly looked the part of a king. David, however, was God's choice. David did not share the same soulish charisma as Saul. David would never have won any popular election. From a human point of view, David possessed no outstanding qualities. Why then did the

Lord choose David? Was it because he was perfect and sinless? NO. Instead, we are told that God found something in David that he did not find in anyone else. How insightful! The Lord is always looking for individuals, in every age, who can serve him per his purpose.

Consider how, when the time came for the Lord to come to this earth and live as man, who did he find to become the mother of Jesus? Was it a woman of means? Someone from a well-known family who was part of Jerusalem "high society"? No, but instead he chose Mary—a peasant girl who came from the despised town of Nazareth. Among the tens of thousands of young women who were living in the land of Israel during those days, it was Mary whom the Lord found and chose as the one who would become the mother of the Son of Man.

The question becomes why? Why David? Why Joseph of the Old Testament? Why the apostles? Was David humble by nature? No. One only must recall his response to the insults of Nabel (see 1 Samuel 25). Recall how Nabel's flocks had been grazing nearby David and his men, and consequently, they benefited from an indirect wall of protection from would-be looters and thieves. In time, David asked Nabel to remember this with some show of gratitude. When Nabel rebuffed David, mocking and insulting him, how did David react? Did David turn the other cheek? Did he "take it in stride"? No. Rather, he set off with four hundred men for destroying Nabel and most of his household. If it was not for Godly intersession of Nabel's wife, Abigail, David surely would have carried out the mission.

So again, we ask, what was it that the Lord found in David? It was the disposition of heart in wanting to do all of God's will. The same disposition of heart was found in Mary. Recall the response of Mary to the angel Gabriel upon hearing that she had been chosen to become the mother of the Messiah. *"Behold, I am the handmaid of the Lord; let it be to me according to your word."*

May we pray for grace that we too might someday long to do all God's will, and that the sincerest wish of our hearts will be the same as Mary—*Behold, I am the handmaid of the Lord; let it be to me according to your word.*

We must be willing to do all that God asks us to do, if we want to have the heart of a champion and be a man or woman after God's own heart.

Chapter 7

David and Goliath
1 Samuel 17:58

IN THIS BIBLICAL story about the heart and mind of one of the bible greatest champions, I want to bring out a few points we have missed when reading this story. You can go to 1 Samuel and read the complete story. I will be adding my comments in italics, to let you know as a champion this is what you may want to do.

> Now the Philistines gathered together their armies to battle, and were gathered together at Shochoh, which belongeth to Judah, and pitched between Shochoh and Azekah, in Ephesdammim.
> And Saul and the men of Israel were gathered together, and pitched by the valley of Elah, and

set the battle in array against the Philistines. And the Philistines stood on a mountain on the one side, and Israel stood on a mountain on the other side: and there was a valley between them. And there went out a champion out of the camp of the Philistines, named Goliath, of Gath, whose height was six cubits and a span. *[A cubit is different in some countries, Hebrew has him at 9'9". Greek Old Testament and the Dead Sea Scrolls has him as 6'9". All English Bibles read nine to ten feet tall. This is just to give you an idea of who he was facing. Remember David was a young teenage boy five feet tall.]* And he had an helmet of brass upon his head, and he was armed with a coat of mail; and the weight of the coat was five thousand shekels of brass *[which equates to about 126 pounds; that is more than David's body weight]*. And he had greaves of brass upon his legs, and a target of brass between his shoulders. And the staff of his spear was like a weaver's beam; and his spear's head weighed six hundred shekels of iron: and one bearing a shield went before him And he stood and cried unto the armies of Israel, and said unto them, why are ye come out to set your battle in array? am not I a Philistine, and ye servants to Saul? choose you a man for you, and let him come down to me. If he be able to fight with me, and to kill me, then will we be your servants: but if I prevail against him, and kill him, then shall ye be our servants, and serve us. And the Philistine said, I defy the armies of Israel this day; give me a man, that we may fight together. When Saul and all Israel heard those words of the Philistine, they were dismayed, and greatly afraid. Now David was the son of that Ephrathite of Bethlehem-Judah, † whose name was Jesse; and he had eight sons: and the man went among men for an old man in the days of Saul.

And the three eldest sons of Jesse went and followed Saul to the battle: and the names of his three sons that went to the battle were Eliab the firstborn, and next unto him Abinadab, and the third Shammah. And David was the youngest: and the three eldest followed † Saul. But David went and returned from Saul to feed his father's sheep at Bethlehem. And the Philistine drew near morning and evening, and presented himself forty days And Jesse said unto David his son, take now for thy brethren an ephah of this parched corn, and these ten loaves, and run to the camp to thy brethren; And carry these ten cheeses unto the captain of their thousand, and look how thy brethren fare, and take their pledge. Now Saul, and they, and all the men of Israel, were in the valley of Elah, fighting with the Philistines. And David rose early in the morning, and left the sheep with a keeper, and took, and went, as Jesse had commanded him; and he came to the trench, as the host was going forth to the fight, and shouted for the battle. For Israel and the Philistines had put the battle in array, army against army. And David left his carriage in the hand of the keeper of the carriage, and ran into the army, and came and saluted † his brethren. And as he talked with them, behold, there came up the champion, † the Philistine of Gath, Goliath by name, out of the armies † of the Philistines, and spake according to the same words: and David heard them. And all the men of Israel, when they saw the man, fled from him, and were sore afraid. And the men of Israel said, have ye seen this man that is come up *[they did not know who they had over the inside]*? surely to defy Israel is he come up: and it shall be, that the man who killeth him, the king will enrich him with great riches, and will give him his daughter, and make his father's house free in Israel. And David spake to the men that stood by him, saying, what shall be done to the man that killeth this Philistine, and taketh away the reproach from Israel? for who is this uncircumcised Philistine, that he should defy the armies of the living God? *[David is speaking like a true champion. He knows he is in the army of the liv-*

ing God. He had no fear because he knew who he was in God. A champion, a warrior.] And the people answered him after this manner, saying, so shall it be done to the man that killeth him. And Eliab his eldest brother heard when he spake unto the men; and Eliab's anger was kindled against David, and he said, why camest thou down hither? and with whom hast thou left those few sheep in the wilderness? I know thy pride, and the naughtiness of thine heart; for thou art come down that thou mightest see the battle. And David said, what have I now done? Is there not a cause? And he turned from him toward another, and spake after the same manner: and the people answered him again after the former manner. And when the words were heard which David spake, they rehearsed them before Saul: and he sent for him.

And David said to Saul, let no man's heart fail because of him; thy servant will go and fight with this Philistine. And Saul said to David, thou art not able to go against this Philistine to fight with him: for thou art but a youth, and he a man of war from his youth *[you can see Saul tried to convince David that he should not or could not fight this warrior; but David, having the heart of a champion, would not receive it].* And David said unto Saul, thy servant kept his father's sheep, and there came a lion, and a bear, and took a lamb † out of the flock: And I went out after him, and smote him, and delivered it out of his mouth: and when he arose against me, I caught him by his beard, and smote him, and slew him. Thy servant slew both the lion and the bear (here he is telling Saul that he slew a lion and a bear and he was not afraid of this uncircumcised Philistine): and this uncircumcised Philistine shall be as one of them, seeing he hath defied the armies of the living God. David said moreover, the LORD that delivered me out of the paw of the lion, and out of the paw of the bear, he will deliver me out of the hand of this Philistine. *[Catch what he is saying. I believe this is where we miss the most important thing David said. He said the LORD that delivered him. Let me repeat, the Lord that delivered him. This is so, so important for us to know the Lord is on our side. When you trust God at his word, the inward man becomes a champion knowing that inward man is the candle of the Lord.]* And Saul said unto David, Go, and the LORD be with thee. *[Even Saul knew what David needed to win, and that was the Lord.]* And Saul armed David with his armour, and he put an helmet of brass upon his head; also, he armed him with a coat of mail. And David girded his sword upon his armour, and he assayed to go; for he had not proved it. And David said unto Saul, I cannot go with these; for I have not proved them. And David put them off him. *[What David is telling Saul about his armour is something we should take note of. We can't use someone else's armour. We must develop our own through the word of God. Yes, people can pray for us; but when we are in a fight, we must use our physical action with the spirit of the Lord. To have the heart and mind of a champion, we must be led by the spirit.]* And he took his staff in his hand, and chose him five smooth stones out of the brook, and put them in a shepherd's bag which he had, even in a scrip; and his sling was in his hand: and he drew near to the Philistine.

And the Philistine came on and drew near unto David; and the man that bare the shield went before him. And when the Philistine looked about, and saw David, he disdained him: for he was but a youth, and ruddy, and of a fair countenance. And the Philistine said unto David, Am I a dog, that thou comest to me with staves? And the Philistine cursed David by his gods. And the Philistine said to David, come to me, and I will give thy flesh unto the fowls of the air, and to the beasts of the field. Then said David to the Philistine, thou comest to me with a sword, and with a spear, and with a shield: but I come to thee in the name of the LORD of hosts, the God of the armies of Israel, whom thou hast defied. *[You need to get this. Please read verse 45 again, and listen to what David said. This is what we are missing when we are in a battle. We go to battle physically, thinking we can defeat the devil and his demons. Wrong, we can't do it that way. We need to be filled with the spirit of God. Tell the devil we come in the name of Jesus, the Lord of host. Remember, at the name of Jesus every knee shall bow, Isaiah 45:23/Romans 14:11. A champion knows the word, and they speak the word. It is not how big you are, not how smart you are, not how rich you are, not how educated you are, and not how old you are, but how much of the inner man you are allowing to connect with the spirit of God, who will lead you in victory.]* This day will the LORD deliver thee into mine hand; and I will smite thee, and take thine head from thee; and I will give the carcases of the host of the Philistines this day unto the fowls of the air, and to the wild beasts of the earth; that all the earth may know that there is a God in Israel. *[David is speaking with authority, knowing what he can do, with God on his side. This is what warriors in the army of the Lord do, when you know whom you belong to, you have no fear. His word tells you that he has not given you the spirit of fear (2 Timothy 1:7). See, David did not care how big this mountain was, what he knew was he served a God that was much bigger than what he was facing. This is the heart of a champion, with a mind stayed on the God.]* And all this assembly shall know that the LORD saveth not with sword and spear: for the battle is the Lord's, and he will give you into our hands. And it came to pass, when the Philistine arose, and came and drew nigh to meet David, that David hasted, and ran toward the army to meet the Philistine.

And David put his hand in his bag, and took thence a stone, and slang it, and smote the Philistine in his forehead, that the stone sunk into his forehead; and he fell upon his face to the earth. So David prevailed over the Philistine with a sling and with a stone, and smote the Philistine, and slew him; but there was no sword in the hand of David. Therefore David ran, and stood upon the Philistine, and took his sword, and drew it out of the sheath thereof, and slew him, and cut off his head therewith. And when the Philistines saw their champion was dead, they fled. *[The difference between the two champions was natural and spiritual. David knew he had the spirit of God in him; he won the battle in the spirit before he even slung the stone. The result was Philistine falling to the ground in defeat.]* And the men of Israel and of Judah arose, and shouted, and pursued the Philistines, until thou come to the valley, and to the gates of Ekron. And the wounded of the Philistines fell down by the way to Shaaraim, even unto Gath, and unto Ekron. And the children of Israel returned from chasing after the Philistines, and they spoiled their tents. And David took the head of the Philistine, and brought it to Jerusalem; but he put his armour in his tent. And when Saul saw David go forth against the Philistine, he said unto Abner, the captain of the host, Abner, whose son is this youth? And Abner said, as thy soul liveth, O king, I cannot tell. And the king said, inquire thou whose son the stripling is. And as David returned from the slaughter of the Philistine, Abner took him, and brought him before Saul with the head of the Philistine in his hand. And Saul said to him, whose son art thou, thou young man? And David answered, I am the son of thy servant Jesse the Bethlehemite.

When we learn to be obedient to the word of God, we can walk in the spirit of victory all the time. Yes, there may be days that you think are going the way you want it to go. But the heart and mind of a champion is always ready for the battle.

We must be Empowered by God

One of the most common excuses for not becoming a Christian is the fear of failure to live the Christian life. Besides overlooking the fact that man cannot be saved on the basis of good works (Titus

3:4), this objection neglects the truth that God provided the power to live the Christian life. Before Christ was crucified, He promised the coming of the Holy Spirit to help the believers (John16:13–14). The subsequent events of the Book of Acts supply ample evidence of the fulfillment of this prophecy (Acts 4:7, 33; 6:8).

The power of the Holy Spirit was not designed solely for the first-century church. Rather, all Christians are indwelt by the spirit and thus have His power available (1 Corinthians 6:19). However, living the Christian life under the Spirit's power must not be thought of as simply allowing the Spirit to take control while the believer does nothing. The believer still must live the Christian life, though he does it through the Spirit's power. Romans 8:13 tells us "if ye [this is us] through the Spirit do mortify the deeds of the body, ye [us] shall live." It is "ye" (us) who are to put to death the sinful deeds of the body. We are to do it through the Spirit's power. The power that dwells on the inside of all of us.

The Christians who struggles in his own strength to live the life of a champion will fail. He must by faith seek daily the power of the Holy Spirit through prayer and worship (Romans 8:4–5). Described practically, this means that the believer trusts the Spirit to empower him or her in specific instances, such as sharing his faith with others. This is what champions do. They are not afraid. They know whom they belong to, who is working on the inside. Resisting temptation, being faithful. There is no secret formula that makes the Spirit's power available. It is simply a reliance on the Spirit to help. This is what David did in his victory over Goliath. It was not by his power but by the Spirit of God that moved through him, giving him the heart and mind of a champion.

The Heart and Mind of a Champion

Scripture reference: Romans 8:37, 1 Samuel 17:17

"Nay, in all these things we are more than conquerors through him that loved us (Romans 8:37)."

1 Samuel 17:17–46, also the book of Daniel, is talking about the troubles/wars we face daily.

1. A champion has no problem being under authority. We as men and women (believers) of God need to get engaged in the battle, stand our ground and accept the authority that has been given to us. Let the Holy Spirit lead us.
2. God always rewards obedience. A champion sees what others don't see.
3. A Champions asks what other won't ask.
4. A Champion thinks what other won't.
5. A Champion walks by faith.
6. A Champion thinks with the end in mind.
7. A Champion knows his future once he defeats the enemy.

8. A Champion knows he will be rewarded because he has the victory in Christ Jesus, which tells him he can do all things through Christ who strengthens him (Philippians 4:13). When we become what God wants us to be (obedient), we become champions.

The Eight Things a Champion Must Have

1. Faith (Purpose): know why you are a champion or want to be one.
2. Passion: a special love for what they believe in.
3. Position: faith that what they are doing will work.
4. Patience: life is a journey; he must follow the spirit.
5. Protocol: a plan of action on what is taking place or will take place.
6. Self-control: know how to control oneself (the flesh) in any situation.
7. Concentration: staying focused on the mission and not the distraction around you.
8. Prayer life: a prayer life is a must if you want to have a heart of a champion. "The effectual fervent prayer of a righteous man availeth much" (James 5:16).

The first things you must do to be a champion is to accept Jesus as your Lord and savior. Then you will begin to hear God. You may say how can I do that? I am glad you ask.

1. Read, study, and meditate on His word daily (Joshua 1:8).
2. Start up a conversation (pray) (Luke 21:36).
3. Then listen (Romans 10:17).
4. You will be led by the spirit (Ezekiel 11:19).
5. Praise him for he inhabits praises of his people (Psalm 54:6 / Hebrews 13:15).
6. We must stand on his word; we can't go anywhere without someone leading us or we have been led by someone. God set up this system so we can lead others and be led by Him, the Holy Spirit, and the father (John 14:26 / John 15:26/ John 14:16).

God has given all of us a heart and mind of a champion, but we take the seed he has given us and put it in our pocket where it dries up and die. That seed is his word. We must read it daily. We must meditate on it daily. We must believe it. And we must act upon it daily. The heart of a champion knows who he is fighting for and why. He knows what he stands for. He knows where his help comes from. Just like David. We can be like David having that heart and mind of a champion, having the courage to stand up to the devil and his deceitful tactics. Like Daniel in the lion's den or the three Hebrew boys who were thrown in to the fiery furnace. Not buckling under the pressure, we all can learn from these few examples. We are living in a world of flip-flop Christians trying to satisfy man, thinking, letting the devil fool them that man can make America great again. As my pastor would say, they need to stop drinking the Kool Aid. (I will explain Kool aid in my next book entitled *YOU*). I will continue to pray that Christians tap into that champion heart God has given them. We must stand up for what the word of God tells us, and let God do the rest. Just see what happen WHEN YOU ARE obedient. Oh what a mighty God we serve.

Chapter 8

SCRIPTURES ON HEALING

HERE ARE A few scriptures you can read/meditate on when you feel sick or someone in your family or others may need healing. Remember, we need to know what the word of God says when we are fighting the evil spirits. A champion knows where the fight began, and that is in the spirit realm. Meditate on these, get them in your spirit, man. Don't forget you are a three-part being: spirit, mind, and Body. The spirit is the inward man; the mind is your soul, your intellect, your emotions; and your body is the flesh, the house the spirit and mind live in. The three must be balanced for you to truly be obedient to the word of God. If you look deeper, you will find out this applies to anything we do in good or bad life. The three must be in agreement to make things happen or to accomplish things. As a Christian, we must have the spirit bring the other two under control. Why the spirit? Because the spirit is the inward man, the real man.

I know you can go to Bible and read these scriptures. I would tell you to do that. I just wanted to highlight a few of them and let you know, when you are praying for healing, it is good to pray the scriptures. We must always remember, if we have faith in God and his word, believing when we pray, we will have what we pray for as long as it is in line with his word. "To God be the glory."

> And ye shall serve the LORD your God, and he shall bless thy bread, and thy water; and I will take sickness away from the midst of thee. (Exodus 23:25)

> And said, If thou wilt diligently hearken to the voice of the LORD thy God, and wilt do that which is right in his sight, and wilt give ear to his commandments, and keep all his statues, I will put none of these diseases upon thee, which I have brought upon the Egyptians: for I am the LORD that healeth thee. (Exodus 15:26)

> Many are the afflictions of the righteous: but the LORD

delivereth him out of them all.
(Psalm 34:19)

Bless the LORD, O my soul:
and all that is within me, bless his
holy name. Bless the LORD, O
my soul, and forget not all his
benefits: Who forgiveth all thine
iniquities; who health all thy diseases; Who redeemeth thy life
from destruction; who crowneth
thee with lovinkindness and tender mercies; Who satisfieth thy
mouth with good things; so that
thy youth is renewed like the
eagle's. (Psalm 103:1–5)

He sent his word, and
healed them, and delivered them
from their destructions. Oh that
men would praise the LORD for
his goodness, and for his wonder-
ful works to the children of men!
(Psalm 107:20–21)

The angel of the LORD
encampeth round about them
that fear him, and delivereth
them. O taste and see that the
LORD is good: blessed is the
man that trusteth in him. O fear

the LORD, ye his saints: for there is no want to them that fear him. The young lions do lack, and suffer hunger: but they that seek the LORD shall not want any good thing. (Psalm 34:7–10)

The righteous cry, and the LORD heareth, and delivereth them out of all their troubles. The LORD is nigh unto them out of a broken heart; and saveth such as be of a contrite spirit. Many are the afflictions of the righteous: but the LORD deivereth him out of them all. He keepeth all his bones: not one of them is broken. (Psalm 34:17–20)

Fear thou not; for I am with thee: be not dismayed; for I am thy GOD: I will strengthen thee; yea, I will help thee; yea, I will uphold thee with the right hand of my righteousness. Behold, all they that were incensed against thee shall be as nothing; and they that strive with thee shall perish. Thou shalt seek them, and shalt not find them, even them that contend with thee: they that war against thee shall be as nothing, and as a thing of naught. For I the LORD thy GOD will hold thy right hand, saying unto thee, fear not; I will help thee. (Isaiah 41:10–13)

When he was come down from the mountain, great multitudes followed him. And, behold, there came a leper and worshipped him, saying LORD, if thou canst make me clean. And Jesus put forth his hand, and touched him, saying I ill; be thou clean. And immediately his leprosy was cleansed. (Matthew 8:1–3)

Come unto me, all ye that labor and are heavy laden, and I will give you rest. Take my yoke upon you, and learn of me; for I am meek and lowly in heart; and ye shall find rest unto your soul. For my yoke is easy, and my burden is light. (Matthew 11:28–30)

And a certain woman, which had an issues of blood twelve years, And had suffered many things of many physicians, and had spent all that she had, and was nothing bettered, but rather grew worse, When she had heard of Jesus, came in the press behind, and touched his agreement. For she said, If I may touch but his clothes, I shall be whole. And straightway the fountain of her blood was dried up; and she felt in her body that she was healed of that plague. (Mark 5:25–29)

The LORD is gracious, and full of compassion; slow to anger, and of great mercy. The LORD is good to all: and his tender mercies are over all his works. (Psalm 145:8–9)

Thou wilt keep him in perfect peace, whose mind is stayed on thee: because he trusted in thee. (Isaiah 26:3)

UNTO thee, O LORD, do I lift up my soul. O my GOD, I trust in thee: let me not be ashamed, let not mine enemies triumph over me. Yea, let none that wait on thee be ashamed which transgress without cause. Shew me thy ways, O LORD; teach me thy paths. Lead me in thy truth, and teach me: for thou art the GOD of my salvation; on thee do I wait all the day. (Psalm 24:1–5)

Beloved, I wish above all things that thou mayest prosper and be in health, even as thy soul propereth. (3 John 2)

And these signs shall follow them that believe; In my name shall they cast out devils; they shall speak with new tongues; They shall take up serpents; and if they drink any deadly thing, it shall not hurt them; they shall lay hands on the sick, and they shall recover. (Mark 16:17–18)

If we confess our sins, he is faithful and just to forgive us our sins, and to cleanse us from all unrighteousness. (1 John 1:9)

As it is written I have made thee a father of many nations) before him whom he believed, even God, who quickeneth the dead, and calleth those things which be not as though they were. Who against hope believed in hope, that he might become the father of many nations, according to that which was spoken, so shall thy seed be. And being not weak in faith, he considered not his own body now dead, when he was about a hundred years old, neither yet the deadness of Sahrah's womb: He staggered not a the promise of God through unbelief; but was strong in faith, giving glory to God; And being fully persuaded that, what he had promised, h was able to perform. And therefor it was imputed to him for righteousness. (Romans 4:17–22)

But without faith it is impossible to please him: for he that cometh to God must believe that he is, and that he is a rewarder of them that diligently seek him. (Hebrews 11:6)

So then faith cometh by hearing, and hearing by the word of God. (Romans 10:17)

Now faith is the substance of things hoped for, the evidence of things not seen. (Hebrews 11:1)

Humble yourselves therefore under the mighty hand of God, that he may exalt you in due time: Casting all your care upon him; for he careth for you. (1 Peter 6:6–7)

Whosoever shall confess that Jesus is the Son of God, God dwelleth in him, and he in God. And we have known and believed the love that God hath to us. God is love; and he that dwelleth in love dwelleth in God, and God in him. Herein is our love made perfect, that we may have boldness in the day of judgment: because as he is, so are we in this world. There is no fear in love; but perfect love casteth out fear: because fear hath torment. He that feareth is not made perfect in love. (1 John 4:15–18)

Be careful for nothing; but in every thing by prayer and supplication with thanksgiving let your requests be made known unto God. And the peace of God, which passeth all understanding, shall keep your hearts and minds through Christ Jesus. (Philippians 4:6–7)

For this cause we also, since the day we heard it, do not cease to pray for you, and to desire that ye might be filled with the knowledge of his will in all wisdom and spiritual understanding; That ye might walk worthy of the Lord unto all pleasing, being fruitful in every good work, and increasing in the knowledge of God; Strengthened with all might, according to his glorious power, unto all patience and longsuffering with joyfulness; Giving thanks unto the Father, which hath made us meet to be partakers of the inheritance of the saints in light: Who hath delivered us from the power of darkness, and hath translated us into the kingdom of his dear Son: In whom we have redemption through his blood, even the forgiveness of sins: (Colossians 1:9–14)

And ye are complete in him, which is the head of all principality and power. (Colossians 2:10)

Trust in the Lord with all thine heart; and lean not unto thine own understanding. In all thy ways acknowledge him, and he shall direct thy paths. Be not wise in thine own eyes: fear the Lord, and depart from evil. It shall be health to thy navel, and marrow to thy bones. (Proverbs 3:5–8)

I had fainted, unless I had believed to see the goodness of the Lord in the land of the living. Wait on the Lord: be of good courage, and he shall strengthen thine heart: wait, I say, on the Lord. (Psalm 27:13–14)

If my people, which are called by my name, shall humble themselves, and pray, and seek my face, and turn from their wicked ways; then will I hear from heaven, and will forgive their sin, and will heal their land. (2 Chronicles 7:14)

There shall no evil befall thee, neither shall any plague come nigh thy dwelling. For he shall give his angels charge over thee, to keep thee in all thy ways. They shall bear thee up in their hands, lest thou dash thy foot against a stone. (Psalm 91:10–12)

Who his own self bare our sins in his own body on the tree, that we, being dead to sins, should live unto righteousness: by whose stripes ye were healed. (1 Peter 2:24)

He healeth the broken in heart, and bindeth up their wounds. (Psalm 147:3)

O Lord my God, I cried unto thee, and thou hast healed me. (Psalm 30:2)

For it is God which worketh in you both to will and to do of his good pleasure. (Philippians 2:13)

He that spared not his own Son, but delivered him up for us all, how shall he not with him also freely give us all things? (Romans 8:32)

Fear thou not; for I am with thee: be not dismayed; for I am thy God: I will strengthen thee; yea, I will help thee; yea, I will uphold thee with the right hand of my righteousness. (Isaiah 41:10)

Why art thou cast down, O my soul? and why art thou disquieted within me? hope thou in God: for I shall yet praise him, who is the health of my countenance, and my God. (Psalm 42:11)

If ye then, being evil, know how to give good gifts unto your children, how much more shall your Father which is in heaven give good things to them that ask him? (Matthew 7:11)

For thou art great, and doest wondrous things: thou art God alone. Teach me thy way, O Lord; I will walk in thy truth: unite my heart to fear thy name.

I will praise thee, O Lord my God, with all my heart: and I will glorify thy name for evermore. (Psalm 86:10–12)

God be merciful unto us, and bless us; and cause his face to shine upon us; Selah. That thy way may be known upon earth, thy saving health among all nations. (Psalm 67:1–2)

Is not this the fast that I have chosen? to loose the bands of wickedness, to undo the heavy burdens, and to let the oppressed go free, and that ye break every yoke? Is it not to deal thy bread to the hungry, and that thou bring the poor that are cast out to thy house? when thou seest the naked, that thou cover him; and that thou hide not thyself from thine own flesh? Then shall thy light break forth as the morning, and thine health shall spring forth speedily: and thy righteousness shall go before thee; the glory of the Lord shall be thy reward. (Isaiah 58:6–8)

And when Jesus was entered into Capernaum, there came unto him a centurion, beseeching him, And saying, Lord, my servant lieth at home sick of the palsy, grievously tormented. And Jesus saith unto him, I will come and heal him. The centurion answered and said, Lord, I am not worthy that thou shouldest come under my roof: but speak the word only, and my servant shall be healed. For I am a man under authority, having soldiers under me: and I say to this man, Go, and he goeth; and to another, Come, and he cometh; and to my servant, Do this, and he doeth it. When Jesus heard it, he marveled, and said to them that followed, Verily I say unto you, I have not found so great faith, no, not in Israel. (Matthew 8:5–10)

He that hath my commandments, and keepeth them, he it is that loveth me: and he that loveth me shall be loved of my Father, and I will love him, and will manifest myself to him. Judas saith unto him, not Iscariot, Lord, how is it that thou wilt manifest thyself unto us, and not unto the world? Jesus answered and said unto him, If a man love me, he will keep my words: and my Father will love him, and we will come unto him, and make our abode with him. He that loveth me not keepeth not my sayings: and the word which ye hear is not mine, but the Father's which sent me. These things have I spoken unto you, being yet present with you. But the Comforter, which is the Holy Ghost, whom the Father will send in my name, he shall teach you all things, and bring all things to your remembrance, whatsoever I have said unto you. Peace I leave with you, my peace I give unto you: not as the world giveth, give I unto you. Let not your heart be troubled, neither let it be afraid. (John 14:21–27)

And again, I will put my trust in him. And again, Behold I and the children which God hath given me. Forasmuch then as the children are partakers of flesh and blood, he also himself likewise took part of the same; that through death he might destroy him that had the power of death, that is, the devil; (Hebrews 2:13–14)

There hath no temptation taken you but such as is common to man: but God is faithful, who will not suffer you to be tempted above that ye are able; but will with the temptation also make a way to escape, that ye may be able to bear it. (1 Corinthians 10:13)

And Peter said unto him, Aeneas, Jesus Christ maketh thee whole: arise, and make thy bed. And he arose immediately. (Acts 9:34)

But unto you that fear my name shall the Sun of righteousness arise with healing in his wings; and ye shall go forth, and grow up as calves of the stall. (Malachi 4:2)

And in that day ye shall ask me nothing. Verily, verily, I say unto you, Whatsoever ye shall ask the Father in my name, he will give it you. Hitherto have ye asked nothing in my name: ask, and ye shall receive, that your joy may be full. (John 16:23–24)

Verily I say unto you, Whatsoever ye shall bind on earth shall be bound in heaven: and whatsoever ye shall loose on earth shall be loosed in heaven. Again I say unto you, That if two of you shall agree on earth as touching anything that they shall ask, it shall be done for them of my Father which is in heaven. (Matthew 18:18–19)

But my God shall supply all your need according to his riches in glory by Christ Jesus. (Philippians 4:19)

And be ye kind one to another, tenderhearted, forgiving one another, even as God for Christ's sake hath forgiven you. (Ephesians 4:32)

I can do all things through Christ which strengtheneth me. (Philippians 4:13)

In thee, O Lord, do I put my trust; let me never be ashamed: deliver me in thy righteousness. Bow down thine ear to me; deliver me speedily: be thou my strong rock, for an house of defense to save me. For thou art my rock and my fortress; therefore, for thy name's sake lead me, and guide me. (Psalm 31:1–3)

Ye are of God, little children, and have overcome them: because greater is he that is in you, than he that is in the world. (1 John 4:4)

The Lord is gracious, and full of compassion; slow to anger, and of great mercy The Lord is good to all: and his tender mercies are over all his works. (Psalm 145:8–9)

And Jesus went about all Galilee, teaching in their synagogues, and preaching the gospel of the kingdom, and healing all manner of sickness and all manner of disease among the people. And his fame went throughout all Syria: and they brought unto him all sick people that were taken with divers diseases and torments, and those which were possessed with devils, and those which were lunatick, and those that had the palsy; and he healed them. (Matthew 4:23–24)

The thief cometh not, but for to steal, and to kill, and to destroy: I am come that they might have life, and that they might have it more abundantly. I am the good shepherd: the good shepherd giveth his life for the sheep. (John 10:10–11)

Have mercy upon me, O Lord; for I am weak: O Lord, heal me; for my bones are vexed. (Psalm 6:2)

I said, Lord, be merciful unto me: heal my soul; for I have sinned against thee. (Psalm 41:4)

My son, attend to my words; incline thine ear unto my sayings. Let them not depart from thine eyes; keep them in the midst of thine heart. For they are life unto those that find them, and health to all their flesh. (Provers 4:20–22)

And if Christ be in you, the body is dead because of sin; but the Spirit is life because of righteousness. But if the Spirit of him that raised up Jesus from the dead dwell in you, he that raised up Christ from the dead shall also quicken your mortal bodies by his Spirit that dwelleth in you. Therefore, brethren, we are debtors, not to the flesh, to live after the flesh. For if ye live after the flesh, ye shall die: but if ye through the Spirit do mortify the deeds of the body, ye shall live. For as many as are led by the Spirit of God, they are the sons of God. (Romans 8:10–14)

Chapter 9

A SIMPLE PRAYER
FOR OUR NATION

ALMIGHTY GOD, YOU are our mighty fortress, our refuge, and the God in whom we place our trust. As our nation face great distress and uncertainty, we ask your Holy Spirit to fall afresh upon your people, convict us of sin and inflame within us a passion to pray, humble ourselves, seek your face, and turn from our wicked ways. As your word says, and you will heal our land. Father in the name of Jesus, I ask that you grant the leaders of our country an awareness of their desperate need of godly wisdom and salvation in you until sin becomes a reproach to all, and righteousness exalts this nation. Protect and defend us against our enemies and may the cause of Christ always prevail in our schools, in the halls of congress, and our homes and churches.

Lord God, send a spirit of revival and may it begin in our hearts. Remember America, remember the foundations on which this country was built. Remember the prayers of our nation's fathers and mothers, and do not forget us in our time of need. I pray and ask this in the name of our Lord and Savior Jesus Christ, Amen.

www.8anewbeginning.com

ABOUT THE AUTHOR

THE AUTHOR IS a born-again Christian with twenty-two years of military service and a mission to educate this generation on being prepared for the battle. He is a warrior recruiting whomever he can to fight the good fight.

www.8anewbeginning.com

CPSIA information can be obtained
at www.ICGtesting.com
Printed in the USA
JSHW012132130720
6672JS00001B/37